Ladybird  Readers

A History of Ferrari

Series Editor: Sorrel Pitts
Written by Sorrel Pitts

LADYBIRD BOOKS

UK | USA | Canada | Ireland | Australia
India | New Zealand | South Africa

Ladybird Books is part of the Penguin Random House group of companies
whose addresses can be found at global.penguinrandomhouse.com.
www.penguin.co.uk   www.puffin.co.uk   www.ladybird.co.uk

Penguin
Random House
UK

First published 2019
001

Produced under license of Ferrari S.p.A.
FERRARI, the PRANCING HORSE device,
all associated logos and distinctive designs
are property of Ferrari S.p.A.
The body designs of the Ferrari cars are
protected as Ferrari property under design,
trademark and trade dress regulations.

Published by arrangement with Franco Cosimo Panini Editore Spa, Modena, Italy www.paniniragazzi.it

Printed in China

A CIP catalogue record for this book is available from the British Library

ISBN: 978-0-241-36509-0

All correspondence to:
Ladybird Books
Penguin Random House Children's
80 Strand, London WC2R 0RL

Ladybird Readers

A History of
Ferrari

Contents

Picture words

racing driver

team

race

prancing horse logo

racing car

supercar

engine

Famous Ferrari

Do you know these cars?

They are all Ferraris. They are some of the most famous cars on Earth.

This is the story of Ferrari cars.

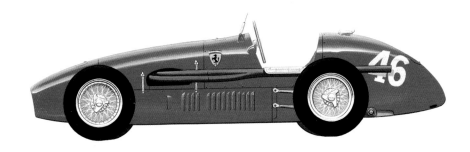

The beginning

Enzo Anselmo Ferrari was born in February 1898 in Modena, Italy.

His father sometimes helped people with their cars, and he taught Enzo to drive.

From the age of ten, Enzo wanted to be a racing driver.

Enzo as a boy

Enzo as a
young man

Enzo Ferrari in 1975

Enzo the racing driver

In 1920, Enzo started driving for the Alfa Romeo team. Three years later, he won the Coppa Acerbo race in Italy.

Enzo in an Alfa Romeo racing car

Enzo won twelve races, and in 1929 he started a racing team called Scuderia Ferrari.

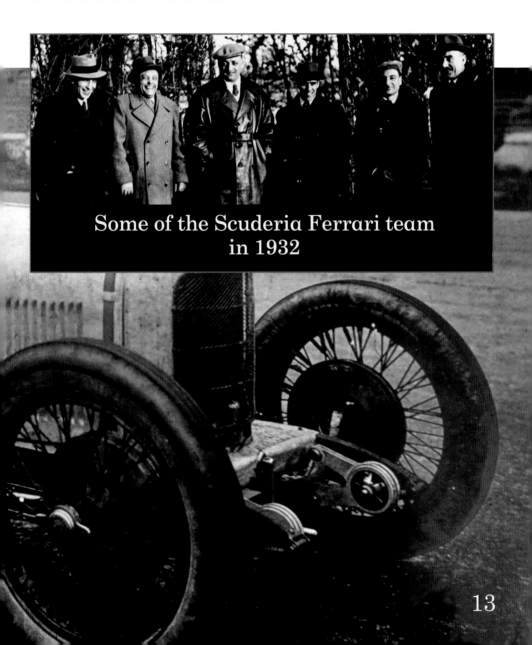

Some of the Scuderia Ferrari team in 1932

The Scuderia Ferrari logo

Scuderia Ferrari's logo was a prancing horse.

The picture of the prancing horse was given to Enzo when he won his first race, by the mother of Francesco Baracca. Francesco had the horse picture on his plane.

Francesco Baracca and his plane

The first wins

Racing driver Tazio Nuvolari won many races for the new Scuderia Ferrari team.

Name: Tazio Nuvolari
Born: 1892
From: Italy
Grand Prix wins: 24
Died: 1953

Tazio Nuvolari

In 1951, José Froilán González was the first driver to win a Grand Prix for Scuderia Ferrari in a Ferrari car.

Name: José Froilán González
Born: 1922
From: Argentina
Grand Prix wins: 2
Died: 2013

José Froilán González driving the
Ferrari 375 at the British Grand Prix

The first Ferrari car

In 1939, Enzo started making racing cars, too.

Name: 125 S
Engine: V12
Power: 118 horsepower (hp)
How fast? 210 kilometers per hour (km/h)

The Ferrari 125 S

In 1947, he made the famous Ferrari 125 S. It was the first car to race with the Ferrari name.

More wins

In 1952, Alberto Ascari won the
Formula One Driver's Championship
in the Ferrari 500 F2.

Alberto Ascari in a Ferrari 500 F2

He won the championship again
the next year with the 375 F1.

Name: Alberto Ascari
Born: 1918
From: Italy
Grand Prix wins: 22
Championships: 2
Died: 1955

Racing cars

In 1957, Ferrari made the 250 Testa Rossa, which won three championships—in 1957, 1958, and 1960.

Name: 250 Testa Rossa
Engine: 60° V12
Power: 300 hp
How fast? 270 km/h

The 250 Testa Rossa

In 1967, Enzo made the Ferrari 330 P4. It won lots of races because it had a very fast engine.

Name: 330 P4
Engine: 160° V12
Power: 450 hp
How fast? 320 km/h

The 330 P4

Supercars

At the end of the 1960s, Ferrari started making cars for normal roads. Enzo called one the "Dino", after his son.

Name: Dino 246
Engine: 65° V6
Power: 195 hp
How fast? 235 km/h

The Dino 246 supercar.

In 1984, Ferrari made the famous Testarossa supercar. Many people remember it from TV's "Miami Vice".

The Testarossa

The white Testarossa
in "Miami Vice"

Enzo also made the Ferrari F40
for Ferrari's 40th birthday in 1987.
It was the last car Enzo made
before he died in 1988.

Name: F40
Engine: 90° V8
Power: 478 hp
How fast? 324 km/h

The F40

The 1970s and 1980s

In the 1970s, Niki Lauda won two Driver's Championships for Ferrari, and Jody Scheckter won one. But after that, Ferrari didn't win the Driver's Championship again for a long time.

Name: Niki Lauda
Born: 1949
From: Austria
Grand Prix wins: 25
Championships: 3

Niki Lauda driving for Ferrari in 1975

Name: Jody Scheckter
Born: 1950
From: South Africa
Grand Prix wins: 10
Championships: 1

Things got bad for Ferrari in 1982, when Gilles Villeneuve died in the Belgian Grand Prix. Villeneuve was a very famous driver, and people were very sad.

Name: Gilles Villeneuve
Born: 1950
From: Canada
Grand Prix wins: 6
Championships: came second in 1979
Died: 1982

Gilles Villeneuve's car at
the Belgian Grand Prix in 1982

The 1990s and 2000s

The 1990s were good years for Ferrari, because Michael Schumacher started driving for them.

Michael Schumacher racing for Ferrari

Name: Michael Schumacher
Born: 1969
From: Germany
Grand Prix wins: 91
Championships: 7

Michael Schumacher is one of the most
famous Ferrari drivers.

In 2000, Schumacher won the first Driver's Championship for Ferrari in twenty-one years. He won it every year for the next four years.

A very happy team

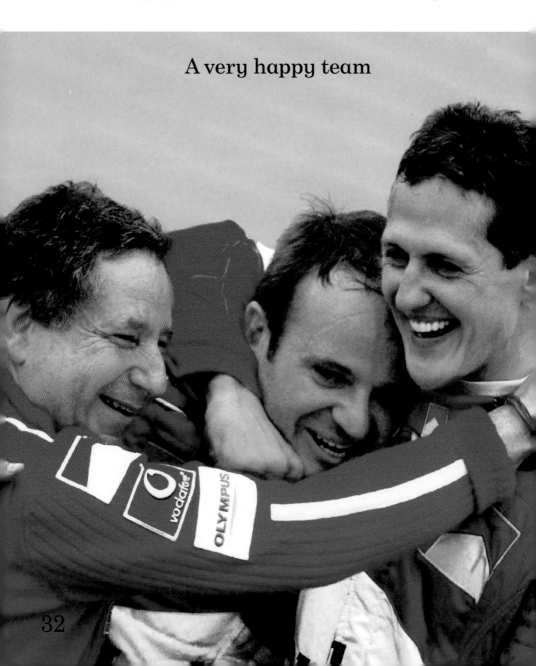

Schumacher
the winner!

More new cars

The Enzo Ferrari was a very fast car made in 2002. It had a new V12 engine, and it looked a little like Schumacher's racing car.

Name: Enzo Ferrari
Engine: 65° V12
Power: 660 hp
How fast? 350 km/h

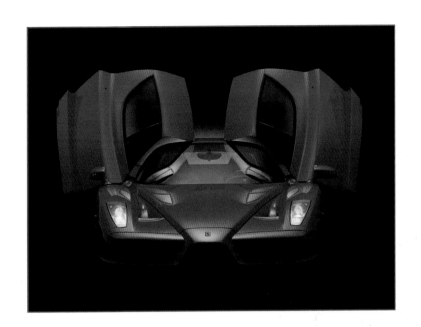

They made the new LaFerrari in 2013. It was Ferrari's fastest supercar!

LaFerrari is a very fast and beautiful car!

Name: LaFerrari
Engine: 65° V12
Power: 800 hp
How fast? Over 350 km/h

Ferrari today

Here are some of Ferrari's other famous supercars. They are very beautiful.

488 GTB

GTC4 Lusso

812 Superfast

Portofino

488 Spider

Ferrari also made the new
SF71H racing car in 2018.

This is the first Ferrari racing car
that must have a "halo"—a metal
bridge over the driver's head.

halo

The Ferrari SF71H

Sebastian Vettel and Kimi Räikkönen drive for Ferrari in 2018. They win lots of races.

Name: Sebastian Vettel
Born: 1987
From: Germany
Grand Prix wins: 52
Championships: 4

Sebastian Vettel at the Australian Grand Prix in 2017

Name: Kimi Räikkönen
Born: 1979
From: Finland
Grand Prix wins: 20
Championships: 1

A History of Ferrari

Ferrari cars are beautiful and fast.
What is more exciting than
driving a Ferrari car?

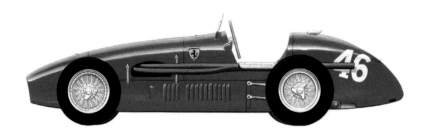

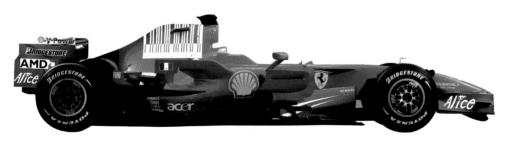

Activities

The key below describes the skills practiced in each activity.

 Spelling and writing

Reading

Speaking

? Critical thinking

Preparation for the Cambridge Young Learners exams

1 Look, match, and write.

1   eng   driver

2   racing   car

3   prancing   ine

4   super   horse logo

1   engine

2

3

4

2 Look at the pictures. Look at the letters. Put a ✓ by the correct words.

1
a car ☐
b engine ✓

2
a race ☐
b run ☐

3
a plane ☐
b logo ☐

4
a supercar ☐
b team ☐

5
a racing car ☐
b supercar ☐

6
a bus driver ☐
b racing driver ☐

3 Talk to a friend about cars.

1

> *What car is it?*

> *It is a Ferrari.*

2 Which is your favorite Ferrari car?

3 Is it a fast car?

4 Is it a beautiful car?

4 **Circle the correct words.**

1 Enzo Ferrari was born in

a 1898. **b** 1998.

2 The Ferrari family is from

a France. **b** Italy.

3 Enzo's father sometimes helped people with their

a cars. **b** children.

4 Enzo's father taught Enzo to

a drive a car. **b** fly a plane.

5 Look and read. Write *T* (true) or *F* (false). 📖 ⭕

1 Enzo started driving for the Alfa Romeo team in 1912.   F

2 He won the Coppa Acerbo race in Italy.

3 He won twelve races.

4 He started a racing team called the Ferrari Squad.

6 **Read the questions. Write answers using the words in the box.** 📖 ✏️

> prancing horse   first race   plane
> mother   Francesco Baracca

1 What was Scuderia Ferrari's logo?

It was a prancing horse.

2 When did Enzo get the picture?

....

3 Who gave it to him?

....

4 Where did Francesco have the picture?

....

Circle the correct pictures.

1 This is the Scuderia Ferrari logo.

2 This is a team.

3 You can fly this.

4 He isn't a racing driver.

8 Read the text. Write some words to complete the sentences about the drivers. 📖 ✏️ ⭐

> Tazio Nuvolari and José Froilán González were racing drivers for Scuderia Ferrari.
> Tazio Nuvolari won twenty-four Grand Prix races for the new team.
> José Froilán González was the first driver to win a Grand Prix for Scuderia Ferrari in a Ferrari car.

1 Tazio Nuvolari and José Froilán González were <u>racing drivers</u>.

2 They both won lots of races for _____.

3 González won Ferrari's first Grand Prix in a Ferrari _____.

9 **Look and read. Choose the correct words and write them on the lines.**

| Ferrari 125 S | Dino 246 | Ferrari 330 P4 | 250 Testa Rossa |

1 This was the first car to race with the Ferrari name.   Ferrari 125 S

2 This car won three championships.

3 This car was named after Enzo's son.

4 This car had a very fast engine.

10 **Complete the sentences.**
Write a—d. 📖

1 Niki Lauda won ....c............

2 After that, Ferrari ....

3 Things got bad for Ferrari ....

4 Villeneuve was a very
   famous driver, ...

---

a and people were very sad.

b didn't win it again for a long time.

c two Driver's Championships
   for Ferrari.

d when Gilles Villeneuve died
   in the Belgian Grand Prix.

11 Read the answers.
Write the questions.

1 Why do people remember the Testarossa supercar?

They remember it from TV's "Miami Vice".

2 _____?

It was a white Testarossa.

3 _____?

Enzo made the Ferrari F40 for Ferrari's 40th birthday.

4 _____?

The Ferrari F40 went at 324 km/h.

12 Read the questions.
Write complete answers.

1 Why were the 1990s good years for Ferrari?

<u>Because Michael Schumacher started driving for them.</u>

2 What did Schumacher win in 2000?

_____

_____

3 How many Grand Prix races did Schumacher win?

_____

_____

4 When, and where, was Michael Schumacher born?

_____

_____

13 Circle the correct words.

1

The Enzo Ferrari had a (new)/ old V12 engine, and it looked a little like Schumacher's racing car.

2

The new LaFerrari was Ferrari's **fastest / slowest** supercar!

3

Ferrari made the new SF71H **racing car / supercar** in 2018.

4

This is the **first / last** Ferrari racing car that must have a "halo".

14 **Do the crossword.**

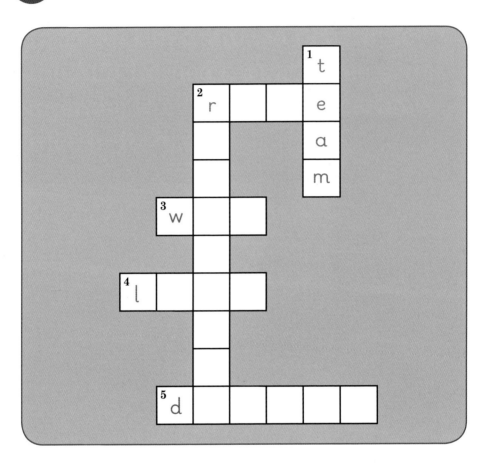

Across

2 Drivers want to win this.

3 The opposite of "lose".

4 Ferrari's . . . is a prancing horse.

5 Sebastian Vettel is a racing . . .

Down

1 Scuderia Ferrari is a racing . . .

2 A racing driver drives this.

15 Write *SV* (Sebastian Vettel) or *KR* (Kimi Räikkönen).

1 He is from Finland. KR

2 He is from Germany.

3 He is older.

4 He won twenty races.

5 He won four championships.

16 Talk about the two pictures with a friend. How are they different? Use the words in the box. 🗨

a

b

race   new   fast   road   roof
supercar   old   racing car

The car in picture a is a supercar.

The car in picture b is a racing car.

17 Write about your favorite racing car or driver. Why are they your favorite? 🖊 ❓

My favorite

Level 3

The Jungle Book

978-0-241-25383-0 ☐

The Red Knight

978-0-241-25384-7 ☐

The Elves and the Shoemaker

978-0-241-25385-4 ☐

Rapunzel

978-0-241-28394-3 ☐

Puss in Boots

978-0-241-28407-0 ☐

Jack and the Beanstalk

978-0-241-28397-4 ☐

Hansel and Gretel

978-0-241-29861-9 ☐

Snow White and the Seven Dwarfs

978-0-241-31955-0 ☐

The Talent Show

978-0-241-29859-6 ☐

Minibeasts

978-0-241-28404-9 ☐

Sharks

978-0-241-25382-3 ☐

Great Buildings

978-0-241-28400-1 ☐

A Great Night!

978-0-241-29863-3 ☐

The Pony School News

978-0-241-31611-5 ☐

The Song of the Sea

978-0-241-36530-4 ☐

Bumblebee and the Rock Concert

978-0-241-29867-1 ☐

A History of Ferrari

978-0-241-36509-0 ☐

Ice Worlds

978-0-241-31957-4 ☐

Where Animals Live

978-0-241-29868-8 ☐

Now you're ready for Level 4!